*sparknotes

TOO LONG; DIDN'T READ

TL;DR

SHAKESPEARE

*spark notes

This 2022 edition printed for SparkNotes LLC by Sterling Publishing Co., Inc.

ISBN 978-1-4114-8061-2
ISBN 978-1-4114-8070-4 (e-book)

Distributed in Canada by Sterling Publishing Co., Inc.
$^{c}/o$ Canadian Manda Group, 664 Annette Street
Toronto, Ontario M6S 2C8, Canada
Distributed in the United Kingdom by GMC Distribution Services
Castle Place, 166 High Street, Lewes, East Sussex BN7 1XU, England
Distributed in Australia by NewSouth Books
University of New South Wales, Sydney, NSW 2052, Australia

For information about custom editions, special sales, and premium and corporate purchases, please contact Sterling Special Sales at 800-805-5489 or specialsales@sterlingpublishing.com.

Manufactured in China

2 4 6 8 10 9 7 5 3 1

sparknotes.com
sterlingpublishing.com

Cover and interior design by Gina Bonanno
Endpapers by Gina Bonanno
Illustrations: MUTI c/o Folio Art Limited

Image credits: **iStock/Getty Images Plus:** TonyBaggett: throughout (signature)
Shutterstock.com: delcarmat: 5, 10, 11, 48, 49; Nicoleta Ionescu: throughout (frame)

*sparknotes

TOO LONG; DIDN'T READ

TL;DR

SHAKESPEARE

Dynamically illustrated plot and character
summaries for 12 of Shakespeare's greatest plays

CONTENTS

dmit it: when you heard *Hamlet* was going to be on the final exam you went out and rented the Laurence Olivier film to cram for it. I mean, why study for five acts what you can watch in two-and-a-half hours—right?

You're not alone here—not by a long shot. A lot of us turn to similar study aids because life is short and time is tight.

And let's face it, even if you *did* read the play, the details don't always stick with you because Shakespeare doesn't always make it easy for you to absorb them. He's fond of setting plays in Italy and giving his characters, both main and supporting, those euphonious names that all end confusingly in "o." He frequently has female characters dress as men and walk around espousing two distinctly different Christian names. And twins!

He often casts his dramas with twins whose identical appearances create numerous instances of mistaken identity. If the characters in the play can't figure out who's who, how are you the reader supposed to?

That's why a book like *TL;DR Shakespeare*—that stands for "Too Long; Didn't Read"—is an indispensable refresher reference for those at sea in their study of Shakespeare. It gives you a handle on twelve of the Bard's greatest plays—six comedies and six tragedies—by parsing his prose and distilling each drama down to its essence.

Each chapter breaks down its play into conveniently concise sections that get to the heart of their elements:

- **A "Plot Overview" that provides a broad perspective on the play's key themes and** describes the drama's forward momentum in terms of its rising and falling action and central conflict.

- A "Main Characters" key that describes the principal players in brief and the roles they play.

- A short list of the main "Themes" and "Symbols" that are the pegs on which Shakespeare hangs his plots.

- A "Key Question and Answer" page that addresses an issue central to the play and deserving of elaboration.

- A page that explains the meaning of the play's ending, and unravels its occasional ambiguities.

The book is illustrated throughout with colorful infographics that further illuminate key plot points and provide you with striking visuals that fix them in the mind's eye of your imagination.

TL;DR Shakespeare is just the book you need to help you "brush up your Shakespeare." Its no-nonsense approach to unlocking the core ideas of Shakespeare's timeless works makes it an invaluable guide for adding a bit more polish to the knowledge you may already have about them. And although it's a handy book to have at hand, it shouldn't be your *only* resource. There's no substitute for the real thing, and it's hoped that this book will drive you to seek out the original plays. So get the basic facts you need here. Then sit back and revel at your leisure in the dramatic splendor of the greatest dramas ever written.

THE TEMPEST

MUCH ADO ABOUT NOTHING

A MIDSUMMER NIGHT'S DREAM

THE MERCHANT OF VENICE

THE TAMING OF THE SHREW

TWELFTH NIGHT

COMEDIES

THE TEMPEST

Genre:
Comedy; Romance

Setting:
An island in the
Mediterranean

Year First Performed:
ca. 1611

The Tempest explores the consequences of European settlement in the New World through the story of Prospero, an exiled ruler who uses magic to restore his daughter, Miranda, and himself to power. To achieve his ends, Prospero must force a confrontation with Alonso, the king who engineered his ouster, by shipwrecking Alonso on the island that Prospero and Miranda share with their servants Ariel and Caliban, and manipulating the romance that blossoms between Miranda and Alonso's son, Ferdinand.

Plot Overview

Climax: Alonso and his party stop to rest, and Prospero causes a banquet to be set out before them. Ariel appears and accuses them of their treachery against Prospero. Alonso is overwhelmed with remorse.

Rising Action: Prospero uses his spirit helper, Ariel, to create a tempest that wrecks his enemies' ship and disperses its passengers about the island. Ferdinand and Miranda fall in love.

Falling Action: Prospero brings Alonso and the others before him and forgives them. Prospero invites Alonso and his company to stay the night before everyone returns to Italy the next day, where Prospero will reassume his dukedom.

Major Conflict: Prospero was banished from Italy and cast to sea by his usurping brother, Antonio, and Alonso. Prospero uses his magic to make these lords repent and restore himself to his rightful place.

Main Characters

 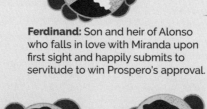 

Prospero: The usurped Duke of Milan and father of Miranda who spends years banished on an island refining his powerful magic.

Miranda: The loyal daughter of Prospero who was brought to the island at an early age and has never seen any men other than her father and Caliban.

Ariel: A magical spirit who works in Prospero's service and who helps to execute Prospero's revenge plot.

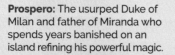  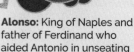

Caliban: Prospero's furious slave who believes that the island rightfully belongs to him and has been stolen by Prospero.

Ferdinand: Son and heir of Alonso who falls in love with Miranda upon first sight and happily submits to servitude to win Prospero's approval.

Alonso: King of Naples and father of Ferdinand who aided Antonio in unseating Prospero as Duke of Milan.

Antonio: Prospero's foolish and power-hungry brother who usurped Prospero's dukedom.

Sebastian: Alonso's aggressive and cowardly brother.

Gonzalo: An old, honest lord who helped Prospero and Miranda escape after Antonio usurped Prospero's title.

Trinculo & Stephano: A jester and a drunken butler who provide comic relief as two minor members of the shipwrecked party.

Themes

Power

Wonder and Magic

Colonization

Symbols

The Tempest

The Game of Chess

Prospero's Books

O wonder!
How many goodly creatures are there here!
How beauteous mankind is! O brave new world
That has such people in 't!

—Miranda
Act 5, Scene 3

Key Question and Answer

Why does Caliban hate Prospero and Miranda?

WHY ?

Caliban sees Prospero and Miranda as colonizers who took control of an island that he felt belonged to him. Caliban ironically mirrors Prospero, who was also violently unseated from power. However, whereas Prospero ended up free but in exile, Caliban ended up enslaved in his own home. Caliban resents going from being the free ruler of the island to being the servant of a tyrannical master. Caliban also resents Miranda for the education she has given him. Miranda describes her efforts as selfless and guided by pity, but Caliban sees Miranda's act as an extension of her father's imperialism.

What Does the Ending Mean?

After Prospero uses magic to split up and torture his enemies, in the final act he lures everyone to the same spot on the island and forgives Alonso and Antonio for their betrayal twelve years prior. The main event that heals the wounds of the past is the union between Miranda and Ferdinand. Finally, Prospero delivers the epilogue and asks the audience to set him free with applause. *The Tempest* marks the last play that Shakespeare wrote by himself, and as such, represents a sort of farewell to his audience. Just as Prospero puts aside magic in the final scenes of the play and prepares for a peaceful retirement, so Shakespeare may have used the play to say goodbye to the theater.

MUCH ADO ABOUT NOTHING

Genre:
Comedy

Setting:
Messina, Sicily (Italy)
in the 16th century

Year First Performed:
ca. 1612

The plot of *Much Ado About Nothing* is based upon deliberate deceptions, some malevolent and others benign. When Leonato welcomes friends to his home, Claudio quickly falls in love with Leonato's daughter, Hero. Don John dupes Claudio and Don Pedro into thinking Hero was unfaithful, resulting in Hero's disgrace. Hero's family pretends she is dead, and this ruse prepares the way for her eventual redemption and reconciliation with Claudio. Meanwhile, Beatrice and Benedick are fooled into thinking that each loves the other, and they actually do fall in love as a result.

Plot Overview

Climax: Claudio rejects Hero at the altar, insulting and accusing her; Benedick, who was most opposed to women and love at the beginning of the play, sides with Hero and his future wife Beatrice, who knows Hero is innocent.

Rising Action: Claudio falls in love with Hero; Benedick, Don Pedro, and Claudio express their anxieties about marriage through jokes; Don Pedro woos Hero on Claudio's behalf; the villainous Don John creates the illusion that Hero is cheating.

Falling Action: Benedick challenges Claudio to a duel for slandering Hero; Leonato proclaims publicly that Hero died of grief; Hero's innocence is brought to light by Dogberry, a local constable; Claudio and Don Pedro repent; Claudio marries Hero.

Major Conflict: Don John creates the appearance that Hero is unfaithful to Claudio, and Claudio and Don Pedro believe this lie.

Main Characters

Hero: Leonato's beautiful and gentle daughter and Beatrice's cousin, who falls in love with Claudio but suffers when Don John slanders her and Claudio rashly takes revenge.

Claudio: A young soldier who falls in love with Hero upon his return to Messina, but who is quick to believe evil rumors and hastily takes revenge.

Benedick: An aristocratic soldier who is very witty and always making jokes with Beatrice.

Beatrice: Leonato's feisty niece and Hero's cousin, who wages a war of wits against Benedick.

Don Pedro: An important nobleman who is generous and loving to his friends, but who is also quick to believe evil of others and hasty to take revenge.

Leonato: A respected, well-to-do, elderly noble at whose home the action is set.

Dogberry: The constable in charge of the Watch, or chief policeman, of Messina.

Don John: The illegitimate brother of Don Pedro who creates a dark scheme to ruin the happiness of Hero and Claudio.

Margaret: Hero's serving woman, who unwittingly helps Borachio and Don John deceive Claudio into thinking that Hero is unfaithful.

Borachio: The lover of Margaret who conspires with Don John to trick Claudio and Don Pedro into thinking that Hero is unfaithful to Claudio.

Themes

Symbols

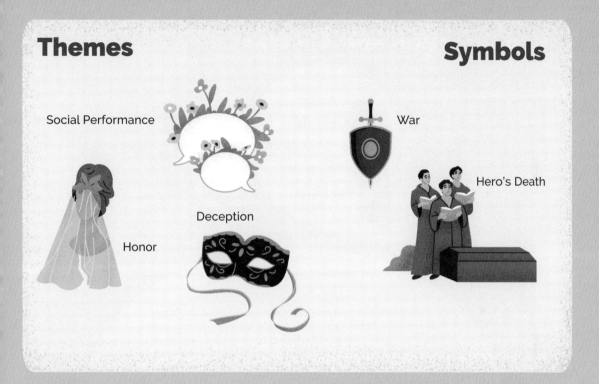

Social Performance

Honor

Deception

War

Hero's Death

*F*riendship is constant in all other things
Save in the office and affairs of love.
Therefore all hearts in love use their own tongues.

—Claudio
Act 2, Scene 1

Key Question and Answer

How do gossip, conversation, and overhearing function in the play?

WHY?

Much of the plot is moved along by characters eavesdropping on a conversation and either misunderstanding what they overhear or being deceived by gossip or a trick. Hero, Claudio, and the rest trick Benedick and Beatrice by setting them up to overhear conversations in which their friends deliberately mislead them. Don John's spiteful gossip makes Claudio and Don Pedro suspicious that Hero is disloyal. The window trick, in which Borachio and the disguised Margaret make love at Hero's window, is itself a sort of overhearing. In this case, Claudio and Don Pedro misunderstand what they see, because Don John has set it up to deceive them. Finally, at the end of the play, the men of the Watch, overhearing Borachio brag about his crime to his associate Conrad, arrest him and bring him to justice.

What Does the Ending Mean?

This final scene brings the play to a joyous conclusion, drawing it away from the tragedy toward which it had begun to move. By blindly marrying a masked woman whom he believes he has never met, Claudio shows that he has abandoned jealous suspicions and fears of being controlled, and that he is ready to marry. He is rewarded by discovering that his bride is actually Hero. Claudio and Hero marry happily, as do Benedick and Beatrice. The deception is revealed, and Don John is caught and brought to justice. Friendship is restored, and the final dance symbolizes the restoration of order and happiness in a world that had been thrown into chaos by Don John's accusation and Don Pedro and Claudio's rash action.

A MIDSUMMER NIGHT'S DREAM

Genre:
Comedy

Setting:
Athens & The Forest

Year First Performed:
ca. 1596

A Midsummer Night's Dream centers around the desire for well-matched love and the struggle to achieve it. The play follows four lovers, a band of craftsmen, and magical fairies throughout a wild, dreamlike night in the forest. After an enchantment devised by the fairy king to humiliate his obstinate queen goes amusingly wrong, the characters fall in love with the wrong people, friendships dissolve, and confusion abounds, emphasizing the ultimate fickleness of love.

Plot Overview

Climax: Lysander and Demetrius quarrel over Helena, and Hermia jealously challenges Helena to a fight.

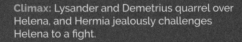

Rising Action: Demetrius follows Hermia, his intended bride, into the forest where she has gone with Lysander. Helena, in love with Demetrius, follows. After the fairy king, Oberon, uses the mischievous Puck to get revenge on the fairy queen, Titania, the young lovers are scrambled up.

Falling Action: Puck reverses the enchantment and sets things right among the lovers. All the right couples are married, and the craftsmen perform their play.

Major Conflict: After Puck sprinkles the magical love potion on the wrong person, the night is thrown into chaos as characters fall in love with the wrong people.

Main Characters

Puck: Also known as Robin Goodfellow, he is Oberon's jester, a mischievous fairy who delights in playing pranks on mortals.

Oberon: The king of the fairies, whose desire for revenge on Titania leads him to send Puck to obtain the love potion that creates so much of the play's confusion.

Lysander: A young man of Athens, he is in love with Hermia, but becomes the victim of misapplied magic and wakes up in love with Helena.

Demetrius: A young man of Athens, initially in love with Hermia and ultimately in love with Helena.

Theseus: The heroic duke of Athens, engaged to Hippolyta, who represents power and order throughout the play.

Nick Bottom: The weaver chosen to play Pyramus in the craftsmen's play, whose foolish self-importance reaches its pinnacle after Puck transforms his head into that of a donkey.

Titania: The queen of the fairies, who resists Oberon's attempts to make a knight of her young Indian prince, and has a brief, potion-induced love for Nick Bottom.

Helena: A young woman of Athens, in love with Demetrius, who thinks that Demetrius and Lysander are mocking her when the fairies' mischief causes them to fall in love with her.

Hermia: Egeus's daughter, a young woman of Athens who is in love with Lysander and is a childhood friend of Helena.

Egeus: Hermia's father, who complains to Theseus about his daughter's refusal to marry Demetrius.

Hippolyta: The legendary queen of the Amazons, engaged to Theseus.

Themes

Symbols

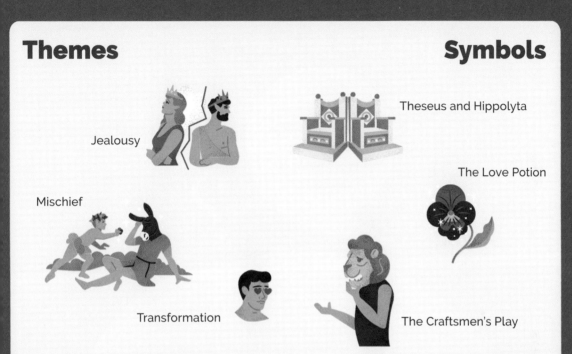

Jealousy

Mischief

Transformation

Theseus and Hippolyta

The Love Potion

The Craftsmen's Play

hings base and vile, holding no quantity,
Love can transpose to form and dignity.
Love looks not with the eyes, but with the mind,
And therefore is winged Cupid painted blind.

—Helena
Act 1, Scene 1

Key Question and Answer

What causes the animosity between Hermia and Helena?

WHY
?

Hermia and Helena's close friendship comes under strain when Demetrius turns his amorous gaze from Helena to Hermia, and Lysander also pursues Hermia. Later, Lysander, charmed by fairy magic, abandons Hermia and pursues Helena instead. This reversal induces Hermia to rage and causes great torment for Helena. The friends' heightened emotions cause them to argue. Although fairy mischief amplifies the animosity between Hermia and Helena, it's important to emphasize that this animosity originated with Demetrius, whose inconstancy first drove a wedge between the two women.

What Does the Ending Mean?

Theseus and Hippolyta discover the sleeping lovers in the forest and take them back to Athens to be married—Demetrius now loves Helena, and Lysander now loves Hermia. After the group wedding, the lovers watch Bottom and his fellow craftsmen perform their play, a fumbling, hilarious version of the story of Pyramus and Thisbe. When the play is completed, the lovers go to bed; the fairies briefly emerge to bless the sleeping couples with a protective charm and then disappear. Only Puck remains, to ask the audience for their forgiveness and approval and to urge them to remember the play as though it had all been a dream.

THE MERCHANT OF VENICE

Genre:
Comedy

Setting:
Italy in the
16th century

Year First Performed:
ca. 1598

The Merchant of Venice tells the story of Bassanio, who wants to court Portia and marry her to gain the financial means to pay back his debt to Antonio, and Shylock, who wants revenge on Antonio for lending money without interest and for his anti-Semitic insults. The play is sometimes categorized as a "problem play," a designation coined in the late nineteenth century in reference to those of Shakespeare's plays with elements of both comedy and tragedy. In the problem plays, comedy often veers sharply into tragedy—in this case, in the final act, when Shylock is forced to relinquish his wealth and convert from his ancestral Judaism to Christianity.

Plot Overview

Climax: Shylock makes the case for his right to collect Antonio's flesh, but Portia, disguised as a man of law, intervenes on Antonio's behalf, and turns the tables on Shylock and his vengeful scheme.

Rising Action: On behalf of Bassanio, who wants to court Portia, Antonio asks Shylock for a loan and agrees to give Shylock his flesh should the loan go unpaid; Bassanio wins the chance to marry Portia in a casket game. Then Antonio's ships, the only means by which he can pay off his debt to Shylock, are reported lost at sea.

Falling Action: Shylock is ordered to convert to Christianity and bequeath his possessions to Lorenzo and Jessica; Portia and Nerissa, still disguised, persuade their husbands to give up their rings, then finally reveal their identities.

Major Conflict: Antonio defaults on a loan he borrowed from Shylock, wherein he promises to sacrifice a pound of flesh.

Main Characters

Portia: An intelligent heiress who marries Bassanio, her true love, and disguises herself to save Antonio from Shylock.

Shylock: A Jewish moneylender who is angered by his mistreatment at the hands of Venice's Christians, particularly Antonio.

Jessica: Shylock's daughter who hates life in her father's house and elopes with Lorenzo.

Bassanio: A gentleman of Venice whose love for Portia leads him to borrow money from Shylock with Antonio as his guarantor.

Antonio: The merchant whose love for his friend Bassanio prompts him to sign Shylock's contract and almost lose his life.

Lorenzo: A gentile friend of Bassanio and Antonio's who elopes with Jessica.

Gratiano: A coarse friend of Bassanio's who weds Nerissa and insults Shylock.

Nerissa: Portia's lady-in-waiting and confidante who marries Gratiano.

Launcelot Gobbo: Bassanio's comical, clownish servant.

Themes

Prejudice

Mercy

Friendship

Symbols

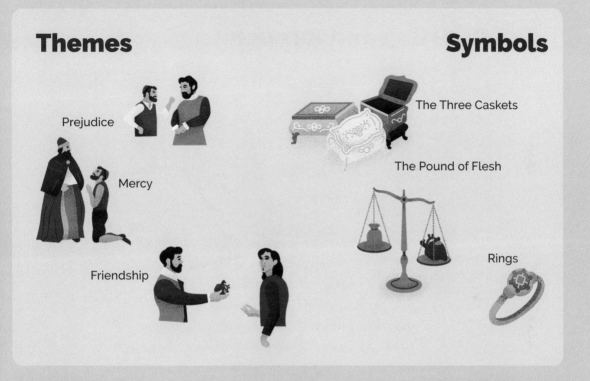

The Three Caskets

The Pound of Flesh

Rings

If you prick us, do we not bleed? If you tickle us, do we not laugh? If you poison us, do we not die? And if you wrong us, shall we not revenge?

—Shylock
Act 3, Scene 1

Key Question and Answer

Who is a more sympathetic character: Shylock or Jessica?

WHY ?

Shylock is spiteful and mean to Jessica, and it is hard to imagine why she should stay with her father. At other times, however, Jessica's escape seems like another cruel circumstance inflicted on Shylock. Shylock is never more sympathetic than when he bemoans the fact that Jessica has taken a ring given to him by his wife and has traded it for a monkey. Nor is Jessica ever able to produce satisfactory evidence that life in her father's house is miserable. Her seeming indifference to Antonio's fate indicates that Jessica may actually be more selfish than the father she condemns.

What Does the Ending Mean?

When Bassanio and Gratiano arrive in Belmont—after having been cajoled by Portia and Nerissa, in their male disguises, to part with rings that the women gave them and the men had sworn to cherish forever—Portia and Nerissa accuse them of faithlessly giving their rings to other women. Before the deception goes too far, however, Portia reveals that she was disguised as the law clerk in Venice, and both she and Nerissa reconcile with their husbands. Lorenzo and Jessica are pleased to learn of their inheritance from Shylock, and the joyful news arrives that Antonio's ships have in fact made it back safely. The group celebrates its good fortune.

THE TAMING OF THE SHREW

Genre:
Comedy

Setting:
Italy during the
Renaissance

Year Written:
ca. 1590

The Taming of the Shrew tells the story of Lucentio's lovestruck pursuit of Bianca, and Petruchio's determination to "tame" the hot-tempered Katherine and become her master. Shakespeare explores these romantic relationships from a social perspective, addressing the institutions of courtship and marriage rather than the inner passions of the lovers. However, it is generally accepted that, by the play's end, Kate has come to accept her love for her husband.

Plot Overview

Climax: Katherine, after succumbing to Petruchio's chastening behavior, finally submits to her husband's will, agreeing to and obeying everything he says.

Rising Action: Baptista declares that no one may court Bianca until Katherine, her older sister, is married. Lucentio disguises himself as a tutor to get near Bianca. Petruchio, looking to marry for money, agrees to marry the sharp-tongued Katherine, and they have a comical wedding.

Falling Action: At Lucentio's banquet, Petruchio wins a bet that the now-docile Katherine is the most obedient wife there.

Major Conflict: Petruchio attempts to "tame" Katherine by asserting his authority in their marriage and overcoming her hotheaded resistance to being his wife.

Main Characters

Baptista: One of the wealthiest men in Padua, whose daughters become the prey of many suitors due to the substantial dowries he can offer.

Katherine: The sharp-tongued and quick-tempered daughter of Baptista who eventually subjugates herself to Petruchio, despite her previous refusal of marriage.

Bianca: The sweet younger daughter of Baptista who is pursued by several suitors, despite being unable to marry until Katherine does.

Lucentio: A young student who disguises himself as an instructor named Cambio to win Bianca's love.

Petruchio: A boisterous, wealth-seeking gentleman who succeeds in wooing and "taming" Katherine.

Tranio: Lucentio's servant who assumes Lucentio's identity and bargains with Baptista for Bianca's hand.

Gremio and Hortensio: Two rival suitors of Bianca who later become friends through their mutual frustration and rejection.

Grumio: Petruchio's servant and the comic fool of the play.

Biondello: Lucentio's second servant, who assists his master and Tranio in carrying out their plot.

Themes

Symbols

Marriage as an Economic Institution

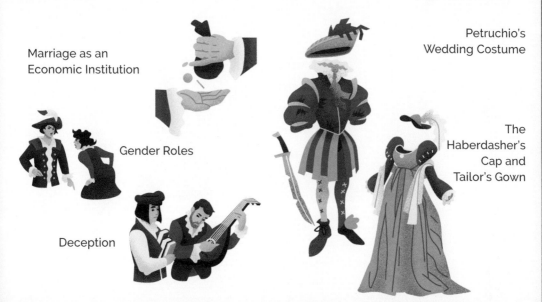

Petruchio's Wedding Costume

Gender Roles

The Haberdasher's Cap and Tailor's Gown

Deception

*T*hen God be blessed, it is the blessed sun,
But sun it is not when you say it is not,
And the moon changes even as your mind.
What you will have it named, even that it is,
And so it shall be still for Katherine.

—Katherine
Act 4, Scene 5

Key Question and Answer

What techniques does Petruchio use to "tame" Katherine?

WHY?

Petruchio proves to Katherine that he can match her quick wit, then he wields his extreme confidence, and his status as a man, when he boldly tells Baptista that she has already agreed to marry him when she has not. At the wedding, he humiliates her by wearing absurd clothing and arriving late. When they reach his house, he pretends he cannot allow her to eat his inferior food or sleep on his inferior bed because he cares for her greatly. As a result, Katherine grows tired and hungry and must depend on Petruchio's goodwill to fulfill her needs, reinforcing in her mind the idea that he controls her. Petruchio couches his attempt to tame Katherine in the rhetoric of love and affection, so it is impossible for her to confront him with outright anger.

What Does the Ending Mean?

At Lucentio's banquet—which is also attended by Hortensio (a former rival for Bianca's hand) and his new wife—the other characters are shocked to see that Katherine seems to have been "tamed": she obeys everything that Petruchio says and gives a long speech advocating the loyalty of wives to their husbands. When the three new husbands stage a contest to see which of their wives will obey first when summoned, everyone expects Lucentio to win. Bianca, however, sends a message back refusing to obey, while Katherine comes immediately. The others acknowledge that Petruchio has won, and the happy Katherine and Petruchio leave to go to bed.

TWELFTH NIGHT

Genre:
Comedy

Setting:
Mythical land of Illyria

Year First Performed:
ca. 1602

Twelfth Night upends conventions of romance and gender roles through the tale of a young woman, Viola, who disguises herself as a man, Cesario, and becomes entangled in the courtship of two local aristocrats. Comic subplots involve the humiliation of Olivia's haughty servant Malvolio, who is deceived by Sir Toby and others into believing Olivia loves him and behaving ridiculously until he's imprisoned for "madness," and the reappearance of Sebastian (Viola's twin brother) who, because of his physical resemblance to Viola, is mistakenly believed by Olivia to be Cesario.

Plot Overview

Climax: Sebastian and Viola are reunited, and everyone realizes that Viola is really a woman.

Rising Action: After a shipwreck separates Viola from her twin brother Sebastian, Viola disguises herself as a man, Cesario, and works for Orsino. A love triangle forms between Viola, Orsino, and Olivia. Meanwhile, Sebastian, who is alive, arrives in Illyria with Antonio.

Falling Action: Orsino realizes Cesario is Viola and agrees to marry her. Malvolio, Olivia's steward, is released from his imprisonment and the practical joke played upon him is explained. Olivia's uncle Toby and Maria marry.

Major Conflict: Viola is in love with Orsino, who is in love with Olivia, who is in love with Viola's male disguise, Cesario.

Main Characters

Viola: The play's protagonist who disguises herself as a young man, calling herself "Cesario," and falls in love with Orsino—even as Olivia, the woman Orsino is courting, falls in love with Cesario.

Orsino: A powerful nobleman who is lovesick for Olivia, but becomes more and more fond of his new page boy, Cesario, who is actually Viola.

Olivia: A beautiful and noble Illyrian lady who is courted by Orsino and Sir Andrew, but who pines for Cesario.

Sebastian: Viola's lost twin brother who arrives in Illyria to find that many people mistake him for Cesario.

Malvolio: The steward in Olivia's household whose haughty attitude earns him the enmity of Sir Toby, Sir Andrew, and Maria, who trick him into believing that Olivia loves him.

Feste: The clown, or fool, of Olivia's household.

Sir Toby: Olivia's rowdy uncle who finds an ally, and eventually a mate, in Maria.

Maria: Olivia's clever, daring young waiting-gentlewoman.

Sir Andrew Aguecheek: A witless friend of Sir Toby's who attempts to court Olivia, though he doesn't stand a chance.

Antonio: A man who rescues Sebastian after the shipwreck and becomes very fond of him.

Themes

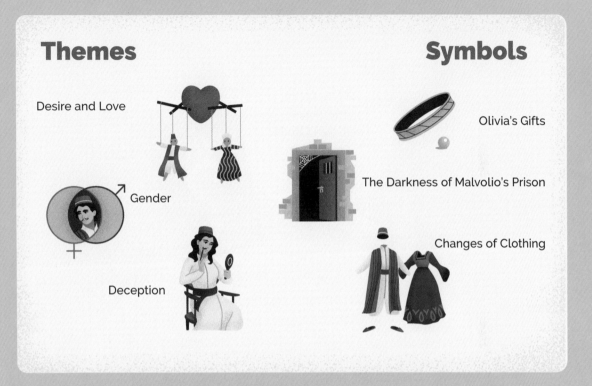

Desire and Love

Gender

Deception

Symbols

Olivia's Gifts

The Darkness of Malvolio's Prison

Changes of Clothing

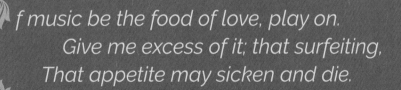

If music be the food of love, play on.
Give me excess of it; that surfeiting,
That appetite may sicken and die.

—*Orsino*
Act 1, Scene 1

Key Question and Answer

Why does Malvolio believe Olivia is in love with him?

WHY **?**

Maria, Sir Toby, and Sir Andrew deceive Malvolio into believing that Olivia is in love with him by forging love letters from Olivia to Malvolio. Malvolio is indeed fooled by the forged love letters, and he fantasizes about living a luxurious life and bossing around individuals like Sir Toby and Maria when he becomes Olivia's husband. While Malvolio is presented as naïve and egotistical for believing that Olivia could be in love with him, he becomes an increasingly pitiable figure as he follows the directions in the forged love letters and makes a fool of himself to get Olivia's attention.

What Does the Ending Mean?

Viola and Sebastian's reunion resolves the various confusions and deceptions amongst the *Twelfth Night* characters and restores society-approved marriages and class distinctions. When Viola is revealed to be a noblewoman and not a servant boy, Orsino quickly transfers his affections from Olivia to Viola, but he continues referring to Viola as "Cesario" and "boy," possibly revealing that he actually loves the masculine Viola. While Orsino can satisfy his homosexual attraction in a way that is socially acceptable for the time period, Antonio's apparent love for Sebastian is left unsatisfied as Sebastian marries Olivia. Malvolio's end is similarly unsatisfactory as he becomes enraged at having been tricked with forged love letters, and he storms off the stage, complicating what is otherwise supposed to be a joyful conclusion.

ROMEO AND JULIET

JULIUS CAESAR

MACBETH

HAMLET

KING LEAR

OTHELLO

TRAGEDIES

ROMEO AND JULIET

Genre:
Tragedy

Setting:
Verona, Italy

Year First Performed:
ca. 1596

Romeo and Juliet is a play about the conflict between the main characters' love, with its transformative power, and the darkness, hatred, and selfishness represented by their families' feud. The two teenaged lovers, Romeo and Juliet, fall in love the first time they see each other, but their families' feud requires that they remain enemies. Despite the couple's secret marriage, tensions between the families escalate. Ultimately, the characters' love does resolve the feud, but comes at the price of their lives.

Plot Overview

Climax: Romeo kills Tybalt (a Capulet) after Tybalt kills Mercutio (a friend of Romeo's), and Romeo is banished from Verona.

Rising Action: Romeo and Juliet meet at the Capulet party and fall in love, then secretly marry each other.

Falling Action: Juliet fakes her death to escape marriage to Paris. Romeo kills himself upon learning that Juliet is "dead," and Juliet then kills herself upon waking and discovering Romeo's corpse.

Major Conflict: Romeo and Juliet struggle against the fighting between the Montagues and Capulets.

Main Characters

Romeo: A young Montague who is impulsive and immature, but also idealistic and passionate.

Juliet: A young Capulet who grows up quickly upon falling in love with Romeo.

Mercutio: A kinsman to the Prince, and Romeo's witty and hotheaded friend.

Paris: A kinsman of the Prince, and the suitor of Juliet most preferred by the Capulets.

Tybalt: Juliet's vain, violent cousin.

Benvolio: Romeo's cousin and thoughtful friend.

The Nurse: The woman who has cared for Juliet her entire life, and who often provides comic relief.

Friar Lawrence: A kind Franciscan friar who secretly marries Romeo and Juliet.

Themes

Love

Fate

Violence

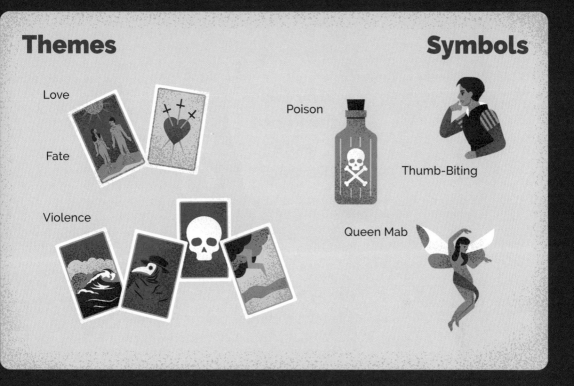

Symbols

Poison

Thumb-Biting

Queen Mab

y only love sprung from my only hate,
Too early seen unknown, and known too late!
Prodigious birth of love is it to me
That I must love a loathed enemy.

—Juliet
Act 1, Scene 5

Key Question and Answer

Why does the Prince exile Romeo?

WHY
?

Normally, in Verona society, someone who commits murder would be put to death himself. Hoping the Prince will see that Romeo rightfully killed Tybalt for killing Mercutio, Montague, Romeo's father, explains, "His fault concludes but what the law should end, / The life of Tybalt." The Prince apparently partially agrees, for instead of sentencing Romeo to death, he merely exiles Romeo for the murder of Tybalt.

What Does the Ending Mean?

At the end of *Romeo and Juliet*, Juliet drinks a potion that puts her in a deathlike trance. Although her feigned death and entombment allows her to escape her unwanted marriage to Paris, it is miscommunicated to the exiled Romeo that Juliet is, indeed, dead. Romeo hastens to Juliet's tomb, and in his grief he kills himself by drinking poison. Moments later Juliet wakes, and, finding Romeo dead, plunges his sword into her breast. At the play's end, the love they share and the violence that separates them become one and the same. Their deaths bring an end to their families' feud, but this peace may only be temporary.

JULIUS CAESAR

Genre:
Tragedy

Setting:
Ancient Rome

Year First Performed:
ca. 1599

Julius Caesar tells the story of how the Roman Republic came to its end. Julius Caesar, ruling as a dictator and soon to be crowned as a king, threatens the Republican government. In assassinating Caesar, Brutus thinks that he is striking a blow for Republican ideals and doing what is best for Rome, but Cassius and the other conspirators have manipulated him. Caesar's murder unleashes a brutal civil war in which the self-interest and power of the warring parties are all that matter.

Plot Overview

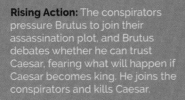

Climax: In his eulogy Mark Antony juxtaposes Caesar's accomplishments, his generous will, and his corpse's brutal wounds with the repeated statement that "Brutus is an honorable man," persuading the Romans that Brutus and his co-conspirators aren't honorable at all.

Rising Action: The conspirators pressure Brutus to join their assassination plot, and Brutus debates whether he can trust Caesar, fearing what will happen if Caesar becomes king. He joins the conspirators and kills Caesar.

Falling Action: Rome plunges into a civil war, and Brutus's men and Antony and Octavius's troops battle each other; Brutus kills himself upon recognizing that his side is doomed, and Antony and Octavius discover his corpse.

Major Conflict: The tension in *Julius Caesar* comes from the question of whether Caesar's position in power is ethically acceptable or not, and whether men of good conscience can allow a man like Caesar to hold such power over the Roman citizens.

Main Characters

Julius Caesar: A great Roman general and senator, who is seduced by the populace's increasing idolization of his image, and ignores ill omens against his life.

Mark Antony: Impulsive and skilled, he persuades the conspirators that he is on their side, then turns on them to gain political power.

Octavius: Caesar's adopted son and appointed successor, he joins with Antony and sets off to fight Cassius and Brutus.

Calpurnia: Caesar's wife, who invests great authority in omens and portents.

Brutus: The play's tragic hero, whose inflexible sense of honor makes it easy for Caesar's enemies to manipulate him into believing that Caesar must die in order to preserve Rome.

Cassius: A talented general, he resents how Caesar has become a god-like figure and manipulates Brutus to believe that Caesar must die.

Casca: A public figure opposed to Caesar's rise to power.

Portia: Brutus's wife, who is accustomed to being his confidante and becomes upset to find Brutus so reluctant to speak his mind.

Themes

Power

Honor

Fate

Symbols

Women and Wives

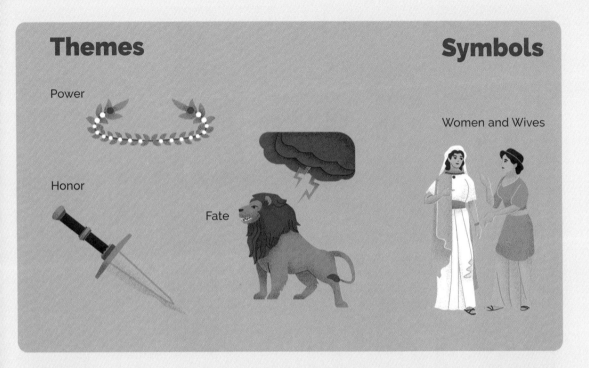

For let the gods so speed as I love
The name of honor more than I fear death.

—Brutus
Act 1, Scene 2

Key Question and Answer

Why does Brutus allow Antony to speak at Caesar's funeral?

WHY ?

Brutus allows Antony to speak at Caesar's funeral in the hopes that doing so will work to the conspirators' benefit. Brutus plans to make a speech to the Roman people, outlining the reasons for Caesar's death, and he tells Antony that he can speak afterward. Brutus instructs Antony to speak well of the conspirators. Although Brutus's words temporarily win the crowd's sympathies, Antony goes on to deliver a moving speech full of masterful rhetoric that quickly turns the Roman people against the conspirators, leading to a riot and, later, war.

What Does the Ending Mean?

The final act of *Julius Caesar* features a battle between the military forces of Brutus and Cassius and those of Antony and Octavius. When Antony and Octavius gain the upper hand, Cassius chooses to kill himself rather than be captured, and Brutus soon follows suit, asking one of his men to hold his sword while he impales himself on it. Finally, Caesar can rest satisfied, he says as he dies. After Brutus's death, Antony and Octavius give short speeches in praise of Brutus, indicating that he was the only conspirator who acted for the good of Rome and concluding that Brutus was indeed an honorable man. Despite their celebration of Brutus's honor, the two men still implicitly condemn the murder to which Brutus's commitment to Rome led him. Octavius orders that Brutus be buried in the most honorable way, and the men depart to celebrate their victory.

MACBETH

Genre:
Tragedy

Setting:
Scotland

Year First Performed:
ca. 1606

Macbeth is a tragedy that tells the story of a general whose thirst for power causes him to abandon his morals and bring about the near destruction of the kingdom he seeks to rule. At first, Macbeth debates whether he will violently seize power, and then struggles with Lady Macbeth as she urges him to kill Duncan, the good King of Scotland. Once Macbeth embraces his ambition and murders Duncan, he struggles against his confederates, Banquo and Macduff, who challenge his authority, and he continues to murder his subjects to avoid the consequences of his first crime. Ultimately, Macbeth's overreliance on his belief that he is fated to be king leads to his downfall, since he believes that the prophecies of three witches met in the aftermath of a victorious battle promise him glory. In fact, the prophecies predict how he will be defeated.

Plot Overview

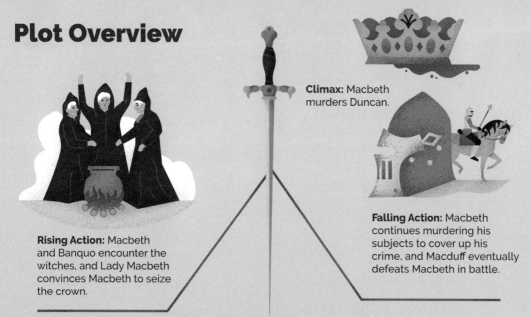

Climax: Macbeth murders Duncan.

Rising Action: Macbeth and Banquo encounter the witches, and Lady Macbeth convinces Macbeth to seize the crown.

Falling Action: Macbeth continues murdering his subjects to cover up his crime, and Macduff eventually defeats Macbeth in battle.

Major Conflict: Macbeth struggles between his ambition and his sense of right and wrong, and also between evil and the best interests of the nation, represented by Malcolm and Macduff.

Main Characters

Macduff: A Scottish nobleman hostile to Macbeth's kingship from the start.

Macbeth: The protagonist of the play who is easily tempted into murder to fulfill his ambitions.

Lady Macbeth: Macbeth's wife, a deeply ambitious woman who lusts for power and position.

Banquo: The brave, noble general whose children, according to the witches' prophecy, will inherit the Scottish throne.

King Duncan: The good King of Scotland whom Macbeth, in his ambition for the crown, murders.

Malcolm: The son of Duncan, whose restoration to the throne signals Scotland's return to order following Macbeth's reign of terror.

Themes

Unchecked Ambition

Guilt

Kingship vs. Tyranny

Symbols

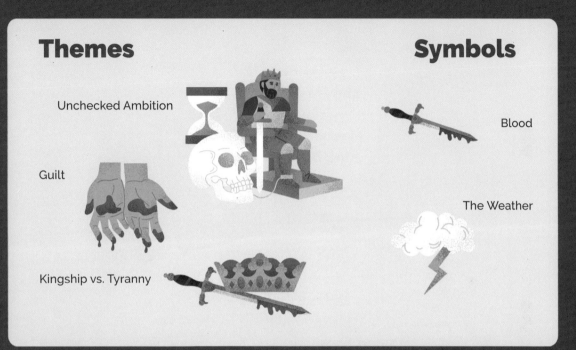

Blood

The Weather

*ife's but a walking shadow, a poor player
That struts and frets his hour upon the stage,
And then is heard no more. It is a tale
Told by an idiot, full of sound and fury,
Signifying nothing.*

—Macbeth
Act 5, Scene 5

How does Lady Macbeth persuade Macbeth to kill King Duncan?

WHY ?

Lady Macbeth persuades Macbeth to kill King Duncan by preying on his sense of manhood and courage. When Macbeth reveals that he has had a change of heart and is no longer willing to kill King Duncan, Lady Macbeth becomes enraged. She openly questions whether he is a man who is willing to act on his desires.

What Does the Ending Mean?

Following the seemingly impossible fulfillment of several of the witches' prophecies—that Macbeth cannot be harmed by any man born of woman, and that he will be safe until Birnam Wood comes to Dunsinane Castle—Macbeth engages with English forces whom Duncan's son, Malcolm, has raised with the support of Scottish nobles. On the battlefield, he is slain by the vengeful Macduff, whose family he slaughtered. Macbeth's severed head is brought to Malcolm by Macduff, proof that Macbeth has been overthrown. Malcolm, now the King of Scotland, declares his benevolent intentions for the country and invites all to see him crowned at Scone. Shakespeare never specifies if Banquo's descendants will take the throne, and thereby fulfill the witches' prophecy.

HAMLET

Genre:
Tragedy

Setting:
Denmark

Year First Performed:
ca. 1600

Hamlet explores questions of fate versus free will, whether it is better to act decisively or let nature take its course, and ultimately if anything we do in our time on earth makes any difference. Once he learns his uncle has killed his father, Hamlet feels duty-bound to take decisive action, but he has so many doubts he cannot decide what action to take. The conflict that drives the plot of *Hamlet* is almost entirely internal: Hamlet wrestles with his own doubt and uncertainty in search of something he believes strongly enough to act on. The lack of resolution makes the play's ending especially tragic: nearly all the characters are dead, but nothing has been solved.

Plot Overview

Climax: Hamlet kills Polonius, a counselor to the king, mistakenly believing he is Claudius.

Rising Action: Hamlet tries to avenge his father's murder, eventually setting up an incriminating play to trap his uncle Claudius into admitting his guilt.

Falling Action: Hamlet returns to Denmark and confronts Laertes, the son of Polonius, at his sister Ophelia's funeral; Hamlet and Laertes fight, and the entire royal family dies.

Major Conflict: Hamlet feels a responsibility to avenge his father's murder, but struggles with his doubts about whether he can trust his father's ghost and its demand for revenge, and whether killing Claudius is the right thing to do.

Main Characters

Hamlet: The title character and protagonist who obsesses over avenging his father's death.

Gertrude: The Queen of Denmark, Hamlet's mother, recently married to Claudius.

Claudius: The King of Denmark, Hamlet's uncle, and the play's antagonist.

Horatio: Hamlet's close friend.

Laertes: Polonius's son and Ophelia's brother, a foil for Hamlet.

Polonius: The father of Laertes and Ophelia, a pompous, conniving old man.

Ophelia: Polonius's daughter, a young woman with whom Hamlet has been in love.

Fortinbras: The young Prince of Norway, whose father the king was killed by Hamlet's father.

The Ghost: The specter of Hamlet's recently deceased father.

Themes

Madness

Doubt

The Mystery of Death

Symbols

Yorick's Skull

Flowers

The Ghost

o be, or not to be: that is the question:
Whether 'tis nobler in the mind to suffer
The slings and arrows of outrageous fortune
Or to take arms against a sea of troubles,
And by opposing end them?

—Hamlet
Act 3, Scene 1

Why doesn't Hamlet kill Claudius right away?

WHY
?

At first, Hamlet doesn't want to kill Claudius because he doesn't feel as determined to act as he thinks he should. Later Hamlet wonders whether he can trust the ghost. In another moment of hesitation, Hamlet aborts the killing of Claudius because the man is praying, and Hamlet worries that his uncle will go to Heaven if he dies while praying. Finally, Hamlet remains unable to decide whether killing Claudius is morally justifiable. Hamlet consistently reasons his way out of committing violence, suggesting that he is conditioned to be a thinker rather than a man of action.

What Does the Ending Mean?

Both Hamlet and Laertes are fatally poisoned during their fencing match, and before he dies, Hamlet kills Claudius. The ending of *Hamlet* leaves it unclear whether the events leave Hamlet's struggles with self-doubt unresolved, or whether they in fact settle his various quandaries. Hamlet has spent the whole play debating whether to avenge his father's death and/or to commit suicide, and the finale effectively enables him to perform both acts. What's unclear, though, is the degree to which Hamlet's final acts are intentional. Likewise, it isn't clear whether Hamlet gets any satisfaction from finally killing Claudius.

KING LEAR

Genre:
Tragedy

Setting:
Ancient Britain

Year First Performed:
ca. 1606

King Lear probes the depths of human suffering and despair in its story of a king who divides his realm between his three daughters. Once Lear's youngest daughter, Cordelia, refuses to flatter him and he divides his kingdom between her conniving older sisters, Goneril and Regan, Lear gains insight into his own nature and realizes his shortcomings. Tragically, this self-knowledge comes too late, at a point when Lear has forfeited all his power. By the play's end Lear has finally learned to love Cordelia without asking for anything in return, only to have her taken from him. All his suffering has been for nothing.

Plot Overview

Climax: King Lear is denied shelter by Goneril and Regan and forced to wander in the storm, driving him mad; Regan and her husband, Cornwall, discover Gloucester helping Lear, accuse him of treason, and blind him.

Rising Action: King Lear cannot understand that Cordelia loves him when she refuses to flatter him publicly. Goneril and Regan actively thwart their father and treat him as a powerless old man. Meanwhile, Edmund schemes to banish his brother, Edgar, and take his place as the heir of Lear's confidant, Gloucester.

Falling Action: Cordelia tries to save her father, but Lear and Cordelia are captured by the English. Edgar duels with and kills Edmund; Gloucester dies; Goneril poisons Regan and then kills herself; Edmund's betrayal of Cordelia leads to her needless execution in prison; and Lear finally dies out of grief. Albany, Edgar, and the elderly Kent are left to take care of the country.

Major Conflict: After disowning Cordelia and dividing his kingdom between Goneril and Regan, King Lear comes to terms with the role power plays in his family.

Main Characters

Cordelia: Lear's youngest and most virtuous daughter, disowned by her father for refusing to flatter him.

King Lear: The aging king of Britain who is used to enjoying absolute power and to being flattered, and who does not respond well to being challenged.

Goneril: Lear's ruthless oldest daughter and the wife of the duke of Albany.

Regan: Lear's cruel middle daughter and the wife of the duke of Cornwall.

Edgar: Gloucester's older, legitimate son, who takes on a variety of disguises throughout the play.

Gloucester: A nobleman loyal to King Lear who, like Lear, misjudges which of his children to trust.

Cornwall: The husband of Lear's daughter Regan.

Albany: The husband of Lear's daughter Goneril.

Edmund: Gloucester's younger, illegitimate son, who resents his status as a bastard and schemes to usurp Gloucester's title and possessions from Edgar.

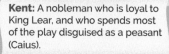

Kent: A nobleman who is loyal to King Lear, and who spends most of the play disguised as a peasant (Caius).

Themes

Self-Knowledge

Generational Conflict

Authority

Symbols

The Storm

Blindness

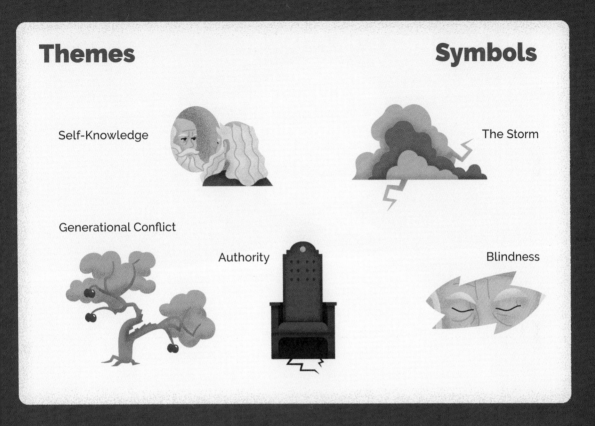

As flies to wanton boys are we to the gods;
They kill us for their sport.

—*King Lear*
Act 4, Scene 1

Key Question and Answer

Why does Cornwall blind Gloucester?

WHY
?

By sending Lear to Cordelia, who is technically a foreign invader, Gloucester may have committed treason against Regan, Goneril, and their husbands. The legal situation is complicated, however, and Gloucester has not had a trial. Cornwall admits he does not have the right to punish Gloucester, but says he *wants* to punish Gloucester, and knows he has the power to get away with the act. The blinding of Gloucester is one of the cruelest and most violent scenes Shakespeare ever wrote. The act emphasizes that the world of *King Lear* is a cruel and violent place, as well as an unjust one.

What Does the Ending Mean?

King Lear ends with a battle for the British throne. Edmund wins the battle for the throne, but is then killed by his brother Edgar. As Edmund dies, he admits that he has sent orders for Lear and Cordelia to be executed. The orders are reversed, but too late; Cordelia has already been killed. Upon discovering that his beloved daughter has died, Lear dies of grief. Generations of readers have found the ending of King Lear unbearably sad. The ending is especially hard to bear because the characters suffer in ways that seem meaningless.

OTHELLO

Genre:
Tragedy

Setting:
Venice & Cyprus

Year First Performed:
ca. 1604

Othello is the story of a noble military general who has enjoyed many successes on the battlefield, but sabotages his most intimate relationship because of mistakes of judgment, his outsider status in society, and his jealousy. Othello's heritage as a Moor with a distinguished leadership position isolates him in Venetian society and influences many of his interactions with others. By the play's end, Othello's misplaced confidence in his saboteur rather than his wife compels him to kill himself, rather than live in a world where honor and honesty have no value.

Plot Overview

Climax: Othello kneels with Iago and vows not to change course until he has achieved bloody revenge for Desdemona's "infidelity."

Falling Action: Iago plants Desdemona's handkerchief in Cassio's room. Iago attempts to kill Cassio, and Othello smothers Desdemona. Emilia exposes Iago's deceptions, Othello kills himself, and Iago is taken away to be tortured.

Rising Action: Iago, Othello's jealous ensign, tells the audience of his scheme, arranges for Cassio to lose his position as lieutenant, and gradually insinuates to Othello that his wife, Desdemona, is unfaithful.

Major Conflict: Othello and Desdemona marry and attempt to build a life together, despite their differences in age, race, and experience. Their marriage is sabotaged by the envious Iago, who convinces Othello that Desdemona is unfaithful.

Main Characters

Iago: Othello's ensign and the villain of the play.

Othello: The play's protagonist and hero, a powerful but insecure general.

Desdemona: Othello's self-possessed wife and Brabanzio's daughter.

Cassio: Othello's young, devoted lieutenant, whose high position is much resented by Iago.

Emilia: Iago's wife and Desdemona's attendant, who is deeply attached to her mistress and distrustful of her husband.

Roderigo: A jealous suitor of Desdemona who is convinced Iago will help him.

Brabanzio: Desdemona's father, a somewhat blustering and self-important Venetian senator.

Bianca: A prostitute whose favorite customer is Cassio.

Themes

Jealousy

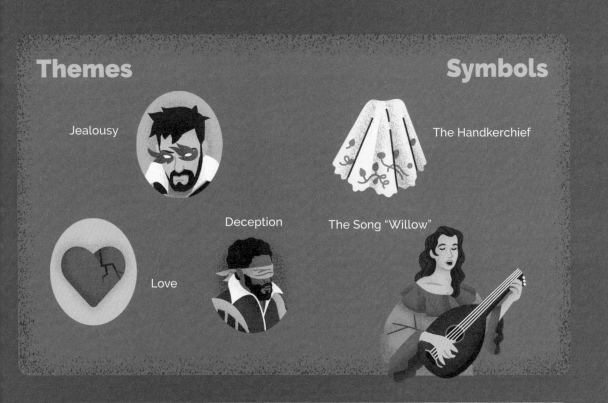

Love

Deception

Symbols

The Handkerchief

The Song "Willow"

h, beware, my lord, of jealousy!
It is the green-eyed monster which doth mock
The meat it feeds on.

—Iago
Act 3, Scene 3

Key Question and Answer

Why does Iago hate Othello?

WHY
?

The main reason Iago gives for plotting to destroy Othello is a suspicion that Othello may have had an affair with Emilia. However, Iago himself admits that he doesn't know whether these rumors are true. Iago also mentions that he is attracted to Desdemona himself. Neither of these reasons seem totally sufficient for just how much Iago hates Othello, and notably, he declines to answer when Othello asks him his motivation at the end of the play. The lack of clear reason for Iago's destructive hatred is part of what makes him such a chilling and effective villain, since he seems to take pleasure in destruction for destruction's sake.

What Does the Ending Mean?

The play ends in a spectacle of tragic violence: Emilia intercepts Othello after he's murdered Desdemona and reveals Iago's treachery. Her revelation is corroborated by information from Cassio and a letter found in Roderigo's pocket. In a vain attempt to prevent his scheme from being revealed, Iago stabs and kills Emilia, and is then taken prisoner while Othello, lamenting the loss of his wife, kills himself next to her. Notably, Iago is left wounded but alive at the end of the play. Cassio is charged with determining Iago's punishment. The ending symbolizes the culmination of the violent forces put in motion by Iago at the start of the play. Iago has been so successful that Othello feels compelled to kill himself. Not only has Othello murdered his beloved wife, he also must face the horrible truth that his suspicions of her adultery were completely unfounded.

COMEDIES

THE TWO GENTLEMEN OF VERONA

Bosom friends Valentine and Proteus bid a tearful farewell on a street in Verona. Valentine is venturing out to see the world, while Proteus stays home, tied by his love for Julia. But when Proteus travels to the Duke's court in Milan at the behest of his father, he falls in love with Silvia, the Duke's daughter, with whom Valentine also has fallen in love. Proteus betrays his friend's plans to elope with Silvia, and the Duke banishes Valentine from the court. Meanwhile Julia travels to Milan disguised as Sebastian, a page, and witnesses Proteus's betrayal of her. En route to Mantua, Valentine falls in with a band of outlaws and saves Silvia, who has fled her repressive father, from the clutches of Proteus. Proteus decides that he truly loves Julia, Silvia's father approves Valentine's marriage to his daughter, and the two couples plan to marry the same day.

THE MERRY WIVES OF WINDSOR

While Sir John Falstaff schemes to seduce Mistress Page and Mistress Ford, both of whom control their husbands' money, Master Slender seeks to woo Mistress Page's daughter Anne, who is in love with Fenton despite her parents' disapproval. Mistress Page and Mistress Ford decide to lead Falstaff on to his inevitable humiliation, and Mistress Ford's jealous husband secretly contributes to his wife's subterfuge by encouraging Falstaff to seduce her to prove his suspicions of her unfaithfulness. The wives subject Falstaff to a series of comic indignities, including hiding him in a basket of dirty laundry that is dumped in the river for cleaning and having him masquerade in a series of outrageous disguises. During one of these ruses, in which Anne and Fenton participate, the couple marries secretly and Fenton eventually is welcomed into Anne's family. All ends amicably for everyone.

THE COMEDY OF ERRORS

Egeon, a merchant of Syracuse, is condemned to death in Ephesus for violating the ban against travel between the two rival cities. But the Ephesian Duke, Solinus, allows him time to raise the ransom for his life when Egeon reveals that he is searching for his wife and a twin son who were separated from him by a shipwreck twenty-five years earlier. Unbeknownst to both, that son, Antipholus of Ephesus, is a prosperous citizen of Ephesus. Confusion ensues when his identical twin brother, Antipholus of Syracuse, arrives in town with his slave, Dromio, who bears the same name as Antipholus of Ephesus's slave. The comic mishaps that follow include Adriana, the wife of Antipholus of Ephesus, mistaking Antipholus of Syracuse for her husband. Emilia, the abbess of an abbey in which Antipholus of Syracuse seeks refuge, eventually reveals that she is Egeon's long-lost wife. Solinus pardons Egeon and the families are reunited.

LOVE'S LABOUR'S LOST

The King of Navarre and his three lords, Berowne, Longaville, and Dumaine, swear an oath to scholarship, which includes fasting and avoiding contact with women for three years—but when the Princess of France arrives to visit the King, the three lords fall in love with her three ladies, as does the King with the Princess. Misdelivered love letters and secretly observed admissions of love eventually compel the men to court the women. The King and his lords arrive at the Princess's pavilion in disguise, but the women, who have been tipped off in advance, switch favors to confuse their identities. After the men leave and reappear as themselves, the women reveal their prank. A messenger arrives to tell the Princess that her father has died, and when she prepares to return to France, the women tell their suitors to seek them again in a year. The play ends with their departure.

AS YOU LIKE IT

After Duke Frederick usurps the throne of his brother, Duke Senior, Senior flees to the forest of Ardenne. When Frederick banishes Senior's daughter Rosalind from the court, Rosalind and Celia, Frederick's daughter, flee to the forest in disguise—Rosalind as a young man Ganymede, and Celia as the poor shepherdess Aliena. Orlando, a young gentleman in love with Rosalind as she is with him, also is forced to flee to the forest after being persecuted by his older brother, Oliver. Orlando joins with Senior; and Rosalind, in disguise, offers to cure the lovelorn Orlando of his affections by taking Rosalind's place and allowing him to act out their relationship. Other couples become entangled in romantic misalliances caused by the confused identities, but ultimately Oliver reconciles with Orlando and agrees to marry Celia; Orlando marries Rosalind; and Frederick repents and reinstates Senior as the rightful duke.

PERICLES, PRINCE OF TYRE

Antiochus, the King of Antioch, offers his daughter's hand to anyone who can guess the meaning of a riddle. Pericles, the ruler of Tyre, tries his hand at solving the riddle but asks Antiochus for more time when he realizes that it references an incestuous relationship between father and daughter. When Pericles returns to Tyre, his friend Helicanus advises him to travel to avoid Antiochus's inevitable reprisal. During one of his travels, Pericles's ship is wrecked and he washes up on the shores of Pentapolis, where he wins a tournament and the hand of Thaisa, the king's daughter. During the voyage back to Tyre, Thaisa appears to die in childbirth and Pericles leaves his infant daughter Marina in Tarsus, to be raised by the governor and his wife. Years later, he discovers that Thaisa is still alive. Pericles, Thaisa, and Marina are reunited at the play's end.

THE TWO NOBLE KINSMEN

Theban cousins and close friends Palamon and Arcite are thrown into prison after Thebes loses a battle waged by Athenian ruler Theseus. Although resigned to their fates, they are both smitten by a glimpse from their prison window of Princess Emilia, the sister of Theseus's wife, Hippolyta. Now bitter rivals in love, the two contrive separate means to escape prison. When Arcite, who has used trickery and disguise to be appointed Emilia's bodyguard, encounters Palamon starving in a forest hideout, the two agree to a fair fight for Emilia's hand. Hippolyta and Emilia convince Theseus, who wants the two men executed, to allow the fair fight to go forward. Palamon, Arcite, and Emilia each pray to a separate god before the fight and their prayers are fulfilled ironically: Arcite wins, but is thrown from his horse fatally after his victory, leaving Palamon to wed Emilia.

MEASURE FOR MEASURE

Duke Vincentio puts Lord Angelo in charge of Vienna temporarily and dons a friar's robes to observe secretly the goings-on in his absence. Angelo, a strict disciplinarian, sentences Claudio to death for impregnating his lover Juliet before their marriage, even though the sex was consensual. Claudio's sister Isabella, who is preparing to enter a convent, pleads on her brother's behalf, and Angelo agrees to pardon Claudio on the condition that she have sex with him. The Duke, in his friar disguise, devises a scheme for Rosalind by which she will agree to sex with Angelo, but then Mariana, a woman once betrothed to Angelo, will secretly take her place, and thereby make it necessary for Angelo to marry her. The ruse succeeds and Angelo is forced to admit his misdeeds. Claudio is pardoned and the Duke asks Isabella for her hand.

ALL'S WELL THAT ENDS WELL

Helena, a woman of low birth, is in love with Count Bertram, who has been sent to the court of the King of France. When the King, whom she cures of illness, offers her the hand of any man of her choice, she chooses Bertram; appalled, Bertram tells her he will never be her true spouse unless she can get his family's ring off his finger and become pregnant with his child, neither of which he will consent to. Helena follows Bertram to Florence and contrives with the help of Diana, a young woman whom he is trying to seduce, to get the ring from his hand and take her place in his bed that evening. When Bertram returns to France, he is confronted by Diana and her mother, who reveal the trap they set for him. Helena tells Bertram that his two conditions have been met and Bertram agrees to marry her and be a good husband.

CORIOLANUS

Following his defeat of the Volscians, patrician Roman soldier Caius Martius is granted the name of Coriolanus. The Roman Senate offers to make Coriolanus consul, but for that to happen he must plead for votes from the plebeians, the lower class that he despises. Although the common people are willing to support Coriolanus, two tribunes, Brutus and Sicinius, persuade them to change their minds, provoking Coriolanus to protest the idea of popular rule. Coriolanus is stigmatized as a traitor and driven into exile. Seeking revenge, he teams up with his Volscian enemy, Tullus Aufidius, and they advance with their forces upon Rome until Volumnia, Coriolanus's mother, begs him to make peace. Coriolanus enjoys a hero's welcome upon his return to the Volscian city of Antium, but Aufidius, now jealous of the attention Coriolanus is receiving, criticizes his failure to take Rome. In the ensuing argument, Aufidius's men assassinate Coriolanus.

TITUS ANDRONICUS

Titus Andronicus, a Roman general, returns from ten years of war having captured Tamora, Queen of the Goths, her three sons, and Aaron the Moor. When he sacrifices her eldest son, Tamora, who is made empress, vows revenge. With her lover Aaron, she has Titus's two sons framed for the murder of the emperor's brother. She then urges her sons to rape Titus's daughter Lavinia, after which they cut off her hands and tongue to conceal their crime. Titus's last surviving son, Lucius, is banished, but he subsequently seeks alliance with the enemy Goths in order to attack Rome. Titus tricks Tamora into thinking him mad, then kills her sons and feeds them to her in a pie. After a spate of killings, Lucius returns as the new emperor of Rome. He has the unrepentant Aaron buried alive, and Tamora's corpse thrown to the beasts.

ANTONY AND CLEOPATRA

Mark Antony, one of the three rulers of the Roman Empire, is summoned back from Egypt and his dalliance with its queen, Cleopatra, to assist his fellow triumvirs, Octavius Caesar and Lepidus, in their quest to suppress Pompey's impending rebellion. Antony marries Caesar's sister Octavia, in a show of solidarity, and the triumvirs ultimately settle their differences with Pompey. When Antony leaves with Octavia for Athens, Caesar wages war with Pompey and imprisons Lepidus. Enraged, Antony returns to Egypt and raises an army to fight Caesar at sea, but loses the battle. Cleopatra asks that her kingdom be allowed to pass down to her heirs, but Caesar agrees only if she will betray her lover. Fearing that Antony plans to kill her, Cleopatra circulates the rumor that she has committed suicide. Antony, upon hearing this, kills himself; Cleopatra, hearing that Caesar plans to parade her as a trophy, kills herself as well.

CYMBELINE

When Imogen, the daughter of the British king Cymbeline, marries the lowborn Posthumus instead of Cloten, his oafish stepson, Cymbeline sends Posthumus into exile in Italy. While there, Posthumus is tricked into believing that Imogen has been unfaithful and he orders his servant Pisanio to kill her. Pisanio, believing in Imogen's innocence, convinces her to disguise herself as a boy and search for her husband. Imogen does but becomes lost in Wales, where she stumbles upon the household of Guiderius and Arviragus, the sons of Cymbeline who were snatched away from him in their youth by Belarius, an unjustly banished nobleman. Through a series of misunderstandings, Imogen and Posthumus each come to believe that the other is dead. Eventually, the confusion is sorted out: Posthumus and Imogen are reunited, Guiderius and Arviragus are revealed to be Cymbeline's sons, and Belarius is forgiven.

TROILUS AND CRESSIDA

Troilus, a Trojan prince, falls in love with Cressida, the daughter of Calchas, a Trojan priest who has defected to the Greek side. Their love is complicated by events unfolding during the seventh year of the Trojan War. Hector, the great Trojan warrior, favors ending the war but is won over by the impassioned Troilus to continue it. In the Greek camp, the great warrior Achilles refuses to participate in combat. Pandarus, Cressida's supportive uncle, arranges for Troilus and Cressida to consummate their love secretly, but the next day Cressida is removed to the Greek camp in a prisoner exchange engineered by Calchas. The death of Patroclus, Achilles's lover, compels Achilles and a gang of Greek warriors to slaughter Hector. Achilles then drags Hector's body around the walls of Troy, and the play ends with the Trojan warriors retreating to the city to mourn their fallen hero.

TIMON OF ATHENS

 Timon, a wealthy and generous Athenian gentleman, hosts a large banquet, by the end of which he has given all of his wealth to its parasitic attendees, much to the dismay of his loyal steward Flavius. When Timon's creditors make demands for immediate payment, he sends his servants to request help from his friends, but they are turned down one by one, forcing Timon to flee into the wilderness. Now a bitter misanthrope, Timon takes up residence in a cave where he discovers a trove of hidden gold. He gives the major portion of this to Alcibiades, whom the Senate had banished forever, to subsidize Alcibiades's planned assault on Athens. Timon spurns Flavius's plea that he return to society, preferring to die in the wilderness. At the play's end Alcibiades marches on Athens and reads aloud the bitter epitaph Timon wrote for himself before his death.

KING JOHN

The play is set in the aftermath of the death of Richard I ("the Lionheart"). Richard's younger brother John is coronated, but the French argue that the throne rightfully belongs to Arthur, the son of John's older brother. It is the first of several family intrigues that prompt, and complicate, war between the two nations. Outside the town of Angers, British and French forces fight to a draw and Hubert, an aide to John, brokers a marriage between Louis the Dauphin, heir to France, and John's niece, Lady Blanche. But at the wedding celebration, John is excommunicated from the Catholic Church, whose representative, Cardinal Pandolf, provokes the French back to war. The English capture Arthur, who eventually falls to his death. John falls ill on the battlefield and dies soon thereafter, leaving his men to face the approaching French forces alone.

RICHARD II

Richard is a regal ruler but unwise in his choice of counselors and detached from his country and its common people. When he begins to "rent out" parcels of English land to certain wealthy noblemen in order to raise funds for one of his wars, and seizes the lands and money of his recently deceased and much-respected uncle, the father of Henry Bolingbroke—a great favorite among the English commoners whom Richard has exiled—Henry raises an army and invades the north coast of England. The commoners, angry at Richard's mismanagement of the country, welcome this invasion and join his forces. Bolingbroke peacefully takes Richard prisoner in Wales and brings him back to London, where Bolingbroke is crowned King Henry IV. Richard is imprisoned in a remote castle, where an assassin acting upon Henry's ambivalent wishes for Richard's expedient death murders the former king.

HENRY IV, PART 1

Henry IV, Part 1 has two main plots that intersect in a dramatic battle at the play's end. The first concerns the strained relationship between King Henry IV and his son, Prince Harry, nicknamed Hal. Harry spends most of his time in taverns consorting with vagrants and other shady characters, among them Falstaff, a liar and thief with an outsized personality. The second concerns a rebellion waged against Henry by the Percys, led by another Harry—nicknamed Hotspur. Believing that Henry has not shown sufficient favor for the Percys' role in helping him to overthrow his predecessor, Hotspur has raised an army against him. Henry summons Harry back to court and compares him unfavorably to Hotspur as perhaps a more deserving heir to the throne. Harry decides to reform his wastrel ways, accompanying his father into combat. Harry saves his father's life in battle and is instrumental in vanquishing Hotspur and the Percys.

HENRY IV, PART 2

The civil war that broke out at the end of *Henry IV, Part 1* continues to rage, and Prince Harry, rehabilitated from his irresponsible youth, is preparing to ascend the throne of the ill Henry. Prince John, Henry's second oldest son, leads the king's army to meet the rebels and, upon convincing them he will meet their demands, arrests them as traitors and has them executed after they send their soldiers home. At the palace in London, Harry promises Henry that he will rule responsibly. Henry forgives him and upon Henry's death, Harry becomes King Henry V. Falstaff, once Harry's disreputable companion, arrives in town hoping to be welcomed into the new monarch's favor, but the king rejects him, telling him he must never come within ten miles of the king or court again. Then, Henry V goes to court to lay plans for an invasion of France.

HENRY V

Henry V, the newly crowned king, gathers troops to invade France and claim parts of the country based on his distant roots in the French royal family. Just before his fleet sets sail, Henry learns of a conspiracy against his life and has the three traitors working for the French, among them his former friend Scrope, executed. The English then fight their way across France, winning battle after battle against incredible odds. Henry proves himself a distinguished commander, exhorting his forces to victory with impassioned speeches. The climax of the war comes at the famous Battle of Agincourt, at which the English are outnumbered by the French five to one. Miraculously, the English win the battle. Peace negotiations are finally worked out: Henry will marry Catherine, the daughter of the French king. Their son will be the king of France, and the marriage will unite the two kingdoms.

HENRY VI, PART 1

Henry V has died unexpectedly, and as the family prepares to crown his heir apparent, word comes of military setbacks in France. The Dauphin Charles is leading a rebellion and he has put Joan, a mysterious woman who claims to be guided by visions, in command of the French army. Back in England, a quarrel between the Duke of Somerset and Richard Plantagenet causes dissension among the nobles. Edmund Mortimer, Richard's father, apprises him of the history of their family's ill treatment by Henry V, which strengthens Richard's resolve to claim the throne as his birthright. Henry arrives in Paris, but the discord between Somerset and Richard affects their military leadership and the English army is destroyed, forcing Henry to sue for peace. The English reluctantly allow Charles to become viceroy to Henry. The Earl of Suffolk persuades Henry to marry the captured French princess Margaret of Anjou, against the advice of other counselors to the king.

HENRY VI, PART 2

King Henry VI marries young Margaret of Anjou, the protégée and lover of the Earl of Suffolk. Suffolk aims to influence the king through Margaret, but first he has to dispose of the king's most trusted advisor, the Duke of Gloucester. Suffolk has Gloucester assassinated, resulting in his banishment. Meanwhile, Richard Plantagenet, the 3rd Duke of York, schemes to claim the throne. Appointed commander of an army to suppress a revolt in Ireland, York enlists a former officer of his to stage a populist revolt to gauge whether the people would support him were he to make an open move for power. The revolt is a success until allies of Henry persuade the people to abandon the cause. Upon his return from Ireland, York announces his claims to the throne, dividing the nobles in their allegiance. York is victorious and sends Henry and Margaret fleeing to London.

HENRY VI, PART 3

Richard Plantagenet, the Duke of York, pursues Henry VI and Queen Margaret to London, where he seats himself on the throne. Henry agrees to York's demand that, after Henry's death, the throne will pass to York, effectively disinheriting his son Edward, Prince of Wales. Margaret, infuriated, abandons Henry and vows to destroy York. Her forces meet York's in battle, and York is brutally murdered. York's sons Edward and Richard raise forces that rout those of Henry, who is captured and placed in the Tower by the new King Edward. In France Margaret enlists the help of King Louis, who is insulted when Edward's marriage to Lady Elizabeth Gray breaks his promise to marry Louis's sister, Lady Bona. Margaret's forces are defeated in England and she is imprisoned. Richard assassinates Henry and realizes that only Edward and his brother George stand between him and the throne.

RICHARD III

Richard, the malicious younger brother of Edward IV, is power-hungry and bitter about his physical deformity. Using his intelligence and his skills of deception and political manipulation, he begins his campaign for the throne. He has his older brother Clarence executed and, after Edward dies, he has Edward's two young sons imprisoned and executed. Richard's reign of terror causes the common people of England to fear him, and the noblemen of the court defect in droves to join forces with the exiled Henry, Earl of Richmond, a challenger for the throne. Richmond invades England with his army. The night before the battle, Richard has a terrible dream in which the ghosts of all the people he has murdered appear and curse him, telling him that he will die the next day. In the battle the following morning, Richard is killed, and Richmond is crowned King Henry VII.

HENRY VIII

Cardinal Wolsey wields considerable control in the court of Henry VIII and has powerful influence over the king. At a dinner at Wolsey's residence, the king meets Anne Bullen and is so impressed with her beauty that he decides to divorce his wife Katherine. A cardinal from Rome arrives with the Pope's decision about whether Henry may divorce Katherine, and although he and Wolsey attempt to convince her to go along with the divorce, Katherine denounces Wolsey as a traitor. When the king discovers that, in fact, Wolsey has been double dealing against him in the divorce proceedings, Wolsey is stripped of his title and expelled from the court. Katherine is demoted to "Princess Dowager" and convinced, that after Wolsey's death, hers will follow. Henry, now married to Anne, celebrates the birth of their daughter, who is christened Elizabeth, and her future greatness is lauded.

EDWARD III

When informed that he is an heir to the previous king of France, King Edward III invades France to claim the French throne. His son, Edward, the Black Prince, is knighted and sent into battle, proving himself after defeating the king of Bohemia. The English win the battle and the French flee to Poitiers with Prince Edward in pursuit. In Poitiers the prince finds himself outnumbered and apparently surrounded, but he achieves victory against seemingly insurmountable odds and captures the French king. At Calais, which has been forced to surrender to England, King Edward demands that six of its leading citizens be sent out for punishment; his wife Queen Philippa persuades him to pardon them. The victorious Prince Edward arrives with the captured French king and the English enter Calais triumphantly.